CW00394826

ACKNOWLEDGEMENTS

Special thanks to Sally Campbell and Colm Bryce for their hard work, support and feedback. Also thanks to Cathy Porter for taking time to meet and discuss Kollontai, and for her supportive comments. Thanks to Simon Guy for help with the design of the book and to Sarah Bates, Amy Leather, Nadia Sayed and Helen Blair for their useful comments and to many more people who helped with discussion and insight. Special thanks to Tom Kay for his continuous encouragement, love and patience; and to my mom, Elise Midelfort, whose memory inspires me daily.

ABOUT THE AUTHOR

Emma Davis is a primary school music teacher and union activist in east London. She is a member of the Socialist Workers Party.

COVER IMAGE: Alexandra Kollontai, circa 1920.
INSIDE FRONT: Kollontai surrounded by Muslim women, thought to have been taken at the Congress of the Peoples of the East in 1920.
INSIDE BACK: The Russian women's naval unit in the summer of 1917, between the two revolutions that shook Russia that year. Photograph by Yakov Steinberg.

Published by Bookmarks Publications 2019
Copyright Bookmarks, 1 Bloomsbury Street, London WC1B 3QE
ISBN print edition: 978-1-912926-14-5
ISBN Kindle: 978-1-912926-15-2
ISBN ePub: 978-1-912926-16-9
ISBN PDF: 978-1-912926-17-6
Series design by Noel Douglas
Typeset by Bookmarks Publications
Printed by Halstan

A Rebel's Guide to
ALEXANDRA
KOLLONTAI

EMMA DAVIS

★ 1: WHO WAS ALEXANDRA KOLLONTAI?

Alexandra Kollontai was a revolutionary socialist who devoted her life to pursuing women's liberation and human freedom. She was one of the leading fighters during the Russian revolutions of 1905 and 1917. Kollontai located the struggle for the liberation of women at the centre of the fight for socialism.

Kollontai lived through a period of history marked by the bloodshed and barbarism of the First World War, and was a fierce opponent of imperialist war. She called for the unity of the working class and oppressed of all nations against their warmongering rulers. A committed internationalist, she was one of a number of socialist women who launched International Working Women's Day in 1910 to celebrate and unite the struggles of women workers across the globe.

Kollontai was a leading member of the revolutionary party, the Bolsheviks, that helped to achieve the immense victory of the working class in the Russian Revolution of 1917. At a time when most countries still denied women the right to vote, she took on the role of Commissar (minister) of Social Welfare in the first Bolshevik government.

Kollontai wrote extensively about sexual and personal relationships and their connection to the struggle for human freedom.

The tragic fate of the 1917 Revolution and the horrifying legacy of Stalinism, which reversed all of the social progress of the revolution, dissuaded generations of activists from looking to socialism as the way to fight for women's liberation.

There is a battle for Kollontai's legacy. Some claim she was simply a feminist who saw men as responsible for women's oppression and thought women should organise separately from men. Others see her as an early advocate of more recent ideas such as intersectionality or privilege theory. While Kollontai's vision of liberation shared many of the same goals as proponents of these ideas, ultimately she was a Marxist and a revolutionary.

Kollontai understood sexism as a result of class society. Women's liberation was bound to the struggle of ordinary people against capitalism.

Today, economic crisis, racism, war and climate catastrophe underline the fact that capitalism isn't working. Far from capitalism delivering liberation for women, sexism is structured into every part of how the system works, from boardrooms to classrooms.

At the same time, we see the continued resistance of women and men to the sexism in the system. Inspiring strikes and movements by women workers around the globe have been at the forefront of this resistance. The need for revolutionary change is as urgent now as it was in 1917. It is for this reason that Kollontai's activism and writings speak to us today.

★ 2:
HOW KOLLONTAI BECAME A REVOLUTIONARY

Kollontai was born in St Petersburg in 1872, when Russia was still ruled by a Tsar (emperor) from the Romanov dynasty. Her family was aristocratic, yet relatively progressive. Her father was an army general and her mother was the child of a Finnish peasant who had become wealthy through trading in timber. Kollontai had a comfortable childhood compared to the poverty that the vast majority of Russians, 80 percent of whom were peasants, experienced.

She described herself as "the youngest, the most spoiled, and the most coddled member of the family" (Autobiography, 1926). Despite her comfortable upbringing, her parents encouraged her to be hard working.

She recalled that from a young age, "I criticised the injustice of adults and I experienced as a blatant contradiction the fact that everything was offered to me whereas so much was denied to the other children" (Autobiography).

Kollontai grew up in a time when Russia was only just beginning to develop industry. Industrialisation happened at an extraordinary rate. In feudal Russia peasants, also known as serfs, had no freedom and were tied to the particular piece of land they worked. The abolition of serfdom by Tsar Alexander II in 1861 broke those ties and opened the way for industrial capitalism. Millions of peasants, including large numbers of women, were forced from field to factory. This fundamentally changed the experience of working life.

Conditions in the factories were horrifying. Women workers had it the worst, often working 14 hour days, earning as little as one fifth of the wages of their male counterparts. They routinely faced sexual harassment and even rape by managers. Poverty wages meant that many women had to turn to prostitution, for which a state license was obtainable.

Peasant women continued to face terrible conditions. Peasant families were fined if their daughters weren't married by the age of 17. Young wives were often expected to have sex with their fathers-in-law. The rule of the Russian Orthodox Church made divorce almost impossible for the poor.

Kollontai's parents rejected much of the sexism of the time, encouraging education for their daughters, but they also expected their daughters to "marry well". Kollontai was horrified when they pushed her older sister at the age of 19 into marrying a wealthier man who was nearly 70. "I revolted against this marriage of convenience, this marriage for money and wanted to marry only for love, out of a great passion" (Autobiography).

When she chose Vladimir Kollontai, an engineer, as her lover, her parents were not impressed and they organised a trip across Europe in the hope of distracting her. In a Parisian bookshop she came across a copy of Karl Marx and Friedrich Engels's The Communist Manifesto and Engels's The Origin of the Family, Private Property and the State. Marx had been an active participant in the 1848-50 German Revolution. Both he and Engels had been leaders of the first International Working Men's Association (IWMA), which united workers internationally against exploitation and for the liberation of the oppressed.

Engels located the origins of women's oppression in the development of class societies. Capitalism—the latest form of class society—reinforced and profited from women's oppression through women's role in the family, their exploitation in the workplace and their lack of property rights. Reading Marx and Engels opened Kollontai's eyes to a vision of a liberated, classless society.

Upon returning to Russia, she convinced her parents to approve her marriage to Vladimir Kollontai. However, married life, and motherhood soon after, did not bring the freedom that Kollontai had hoped for. She recalled, "I still loved my husband, but the happy life of a housewife and spouse became for me a cage" (Autobiography).

In 1894 something changed. Tsar Nicholas II led a wholesale assault on the working class, provoking an outburst of strikes and protests. Kollontai was inspired by the strikes, including the 2,000 women workers who struck at St Petersburg's Laferme Cigarette Factory. She began to work with experienced women revolutionaries like Nadezhda Krupskaya, whose partner was the leading Russian Marxist, Lenin. They taught evening classes for workers, raised money for strikes and smuggled illegal pamphlets.

Her revolutionary activity was creating tensions in her marriage. Vladimir took her to a factory to show her how he was working to improve the ventilation. But Kollontai was horrified by what she saw. The 12,000 workers endured 18-hour days, seven days a week, in stifling factory rooms polluted by textile fibres. Many would develop tuberculosis and die by the age of 30. Far from being reassured, she left the factory even more convinced of the need for a revolutionary struggle of workers against the system. "I could not lead a happy, peaceful life when the working population was so terribly enslaved. I simply had to join this movement" (Autobiography).

In 1896, Russia's first mass strike wave broke out across the textile mills of St Petersburg. Women, 40 percent of the workforce, were leaders in the strikes. Kollontai recalled, "It was indeed wonderful that the politically naïve factory girl, hopelessly bowed down by the harsh, unbearable work conditions, despised by one and all...should be in the vanguard, now fighting for the rights of the working class and the emancipation of women" (Alix Holt, Selected Writings of Alexandra Kollontai, Allison & Busby, 1977, p39).

Kollontai later wrote, "The movement of women workers is by its very nature an indivisible part of the general workers' movement... In all the risings and in all the factory riots that were so distasteful to Tsarism she took an equal part, alongside the working man" (Women Workers and the Struggle for Their Rights, 1919).

In 1897 there was another wave of strikes, followed by a period of extreme repression by the Tsarist authorities. Many revolutionaries were rounded up by the Tsarist police and exiled to Siberia. Those who remained had to operate underground.

It was in this context that Kollontai made the decision to leave Vladimir. She left her son with her parents and boarded a train bound for Europe. She planned to study Marxism and throw herself into the socialist movement.

★ 3: DEBATES IN GERMANY AND RUSSIA

Kollontai spent most of the year of 1898-99 in Zurich, Switzerland studying Marxism and engaging with debates within the German Social Democratic Party (SPD). The SPD, whose ideas were rooted in Marxism, was by far the biggest socialist organisation in the world, with thousands of members. It was a source of inspiration and guidance for socialists across Europe.

As German capitalism expanded, so did attacks by the Kaiser, or emperor, on working class people. The SPD was at the forefront of resisting the Kaiser and was hugely successful, at one point winning 4.5 million votes and the majority of seats in parliament. The SPD's electoral success was accompanied by high levels of industrial action by the new German trade unions, leading to a series of victories for the working class.

The electoral success of the party caused a leading member, Eduard Bernstein, to argue that revolution was no longer needed to create socialism. Rather, it could be won gradually through electing socialists to parliament and improvements made by the trade unions. This fundamentally revised the revolutionary project of Marxism, and would become known as "revisionism". It expressed the gradual, reformist approach that the SPD had in practice, despite their rhetorical commitment to revolution.

Drawing on her experience of the strike waves in Russia, Kollontai was critical of revisionism. She was closer in her thinking to the Polish Marxist Rosa Luxemburg, who was also a prominent member of the SPD, and for whom a revolutionary, working class overthrow of capitalism was the only way of securing socialism. Kollontai and Luxemburg later met briefly in 1901, and Kollontai was inspired by Luxemburg to study Marxist economics.

Back in Russia, Kollontai joined Lenin's party, the Russian Social Democratic Labour Party (RSDLP).

Russia saw the return of mass strikes and riots against the Tsarist regime in 1901. The Tsar clamped down violently, employing huge numbers of police spies, making it nearly impossible to organise resistance. Among those who opposed the Tsar, there was a debate about how to organise in these difficult circumstances.

Lenin and a number of other socialists argued there was the need for a tightly organised, underground revolutionary party. This would enable them to support the most confident workers fighting back, while avoiding arrest.

Other Russian socialists were in favour of a looser organisation, with a closer relationship to the emerging liberal, capitalist class. But this revealed a disagreement about how socialism would come about in Russia. Those in favour of a looser organisation believed that it was necessary to form an alliance with the liberals in order to achieve parliamentary democracy and the development of capitalism in Russia, before the struggle for socialism could begin in earnest.

This debate led to a split in the RSDLP in 1903 between Lenin's faction, the Bolsheviks (majority) and the Mensheviks (minority).

Kollontai agreed with Lenin's position on the need for a tight organisation of committed revolutionaries. However, she was also sympathetic to the Mensheviks and respected many of their leading members. At first, Kollontai did not join either wing of the party. Like many revolutionaries of the time, she would be an active member of both at different times over the years.

In February 1904 the Tsar started a war with imperial Japan over which country would have control of Korea and Manchuria (located within modern North East China, Russia and Mongolia). The Russian state ran a nasty, racist campaign against the Japanese. Thousands of Russian workers and peasants were sent to their deaths.

The liberal, capitalist class shamefully supported the war, and some Mensheviks followed suit. This prompted Kollontai to join the Bolsheviks.

The war left peasant women and children starving, forced to work in some of the most dangerous, low paying factories, or turning to prostitution. There was mounting discontent. Peasant women were for the first time, "leaving their homes, their passivity and their ignorance behind them and hurrying to the towns to find work or tread the corridors of government institutions in the hope of news from a husband, son or a father to stand up for their widows' pensions and fight for their rights... Those who returned to the villages did so in a sober hardened mood" (Cathy Porter, Alexandra Kollontai: A Biography, Merlin Press, 2013, p91).

★ 4: THE 1905 REVOLUTION

The anger and despair over poverty and the disastrous war reached a boiling point in early January of 1905. The strike that broke out at the enormous Putilov arms factory in St Petersburg was, according to Kollontai, "the spark which ignited this rotting nest of universal discontentment" (Porter, p91).

The strike spread across the city, from shipyards to bakeries. By 21 January the whole of St Petersburg was shut down, with no electricity, newspapers or bakeries.

On 22 January thousands of workers, led by the priest Father Gapon, marched on the Tsar's Winter Palace with a petition asking for a constitution and basic democratic rights. Nothing could have prepared the peaceful protesters for the thousands of bullets that fell upon them. Kollontai recalled the "trusting expectant faces, the fateful signal of the troops stationed around the Palace, the pools of blood on the snow, the bellowing of the gendarmes, the dead, the wounded, the children shot" (Porter, p92).

Some 2,000 workers were massacred on what became known as Bloody Sunday. Kollontai wrote:

"On that day he [the Tsar] had killed something even greater, he had killed superstition, and the workers' faith that they could ever achieve justice from him. From then on everything was different and new" (Porter, p92).

General strikes spread across Russia's major cities. Sailors in the Black Sea fleet mutinied. The following months were fuelled by an ever-growing movement by workers, students and peasants against the Tsar, in the face of armed police. Facing chaos at home, the Tsar was forced to negotiate peace with Japan.

Kollontai worked tirelessly throughout the revolution. The Bolsheviks sent her briefly to Finland to help organise workers, utilising her understanding of the language and culture gained from her visits to her mother's family as a child.

During the strikes of the 1890s workers had set up independent strike committees. In 1905 these mass, democratically elected councils, or "soviets" re-emerged, separate from the official trade unions. The entire working class of the capital city was organised in the St Petersburg Soviet of Workers. The working class, despite being a minority in Russian society, was leading the way with new forms of democratic organisation and decision-making.

Women workers were leaders in the revolution and began to challenge their deep-rooted oppression. Kollontai observed, "As the working woman gradually came to understand the world she was living in and the injustice of the capitalist system, she felt more bitter about the suffering she endured, and the voice of the working class began to ring out even more forcefully for her needs to be recognised" (Porter, p94).

Women began to demand maternity leave, crèches and time off to breast feed at work. Kollontai observed that in 1905 there was "no corner in which the voice of a woman speaking about herself and demanding new rights was not heard" (Hillyar and McDermid, Midwives of the Revolution, UCL Press, 1999, p47).

The Bolsheviks, who, up until 1905, had been organising

in secret, flung their doors open to factory workers. The days of operating under the police state were over.

Due to her close contact with workers, Kollontai was invited to join 90 elected delegates at the first meeting of the St Petersburg Soviet in October, chaired by Leon Trotsky. Trotsky was a young, Jewish revolutionary, who had grown up under the Tsar's deeply antisemitic regime. He believed the workers' soviets would be central to overthrowing the Tsar.

Listening to Trotsky had a profound effect on Kollontai. "He had taken the measure of the Soviet, intuitively grasped its significance, and with graphic clarity he went on to trace the tasks of this new organisation of 'workers' unity'" (Porter, p101).

The St Petersburg Soviet called a general strike. The mass strikes and peasants' revolts continued until December 1905. Panicking at the growing resistance and in an attempt to pacify the revolution, the Tsar granted some limited concessions. For the first time in Russia's history a Duma, or parliament, was established. There were elections in which political parties, socialists and trade unionists could participate.

However, the Duma had virtually no real power. Landowners were guaranteed the majority of seats, and all ministers had to answer to the Tsar. Women were denied the right to involvement in the Duma.

The revolution had a unifying effect on socialists, but the introduction of the Duma sparked a new disagreement between the Bolsheviks and Mensheviks.

Initially the Bolsheviks boycotted the Duma, labelling it a "pseudo-parliament" and a retreat from the revolution. The Mensheviks were in favour of limited involvement, as they believed it provided an opportunity for the revolutionary workers' organisation to work with the liberals.

Kollontai agreed that the Duma was a sham, but she also felt workers' organisations should seize any opportunity to raise their demands. She decided to leave the Bolsheviks and join the Mensheviks.

Once it was clear that the revolution was over, the Bolsheviks did participate in the Duma. However, they were clear that socialists should only be involved in the Duma in order to raise the banner of socialism and give the working class a voice. Any alliance with the liberal, capitalist class would cause a conflict of interest over the demands of workers.

The 1905 revolution was a turning point for Kollontai as it was for the revolutionary movement more broadly. It showed the immense power of the working class to raise demands that stretched far beyond the factory walls, to bring the Tsarist regime to the brink of collapse.

Rosa Luxemburg described how the revolution had awakened those previously disenfranchised from politics:

"In a revolutionary period, in the storm of great unsettling class struggles, the whole educational effect of the rapid capitalist development and of social democratic influences first shows itself upon the widest sections of the people, of which, in peaceful times the tables of the organised, and even election statistics, give only a faint idea" (Luxemburg, The Mass Strike, 1906).

Indeed, women workers had proven themselves to be central to the revolutionary movement. Kollontai wrote that the woman worker had "awoken from her slumbers. She was to be found everywhere" (Kollontai, On the History of the Movement of Women Workers in Russia, 1920).

★5: THE WOMEN'S MOVEMENT RISES

The events of 1905 changed everything. For the first time in Russia's history, the question of women's liberation was raised on a mass scale. Working class and peasant women, through their struggle against the regime, were beginning to challenge sexist ideas and practices throughout society.

Middle class women, riding on the shoulders of the working class movement, began to raise their voices, too. Inspired by the suffragettes' fight for the vote in England, the Russian bourgeois women in the Union of Women's Equality appealed to the Duma for voting rights. Their demand was rejected. So, learning the lessons of 1905, they turned to working class women to build a campaign for the right of propertied women to vote.

They promised that if middle class women were involved in the Duma, working class women would also benefit from reforms such as divorce rights.

Kollontai was not convinced that fighting for the interests of middle class women would deliver for working class women. She saw that the new women's movement was incredibly important, and was a sign of the impact of the revolution across society. But she also felt that limiting its demands to the right for middle class women to vote undermined the millions of working class women and men whose struggles had won the Duma in the first place.

The extent to which socialists should be involved in the feminists' fight for the vote was being debated within the socialist movement internationally. In England socialist women were working very closely with the middle class feminists. In Austria socialists were refusing to get involved, concerned that the middle class women would detract from the unity of the working class.

In Russia the Mensheviks wanted a broad alliance between socialist and middle class women, while the Bolsheviks opposed this, seeing middle class liberals as untrustworthy allies who would ultimately side with the Tsar. Kollontai, though a member of the Mensheviks, opposed an alliance with the middle class feminists for similar reasons. However, she maintained that socialists must be involved in the struggle for equality, including the right to vote.

She later wrote, "I threw myself into the struggle between the Russian suffragettes and strove with all my might to induce the working class movement to include the woman question as one of the aims of its struggle" (Autobiography). Kollontai took a lead from the German socialist Clara Zetkin, for whom the question of equal rights for women was non-negotiable. Zetkin insisted that socialists' demands must extend beyond the right of middle class women to vote, to the right of all people to vote—universal suffrage.

Many working class women had grown in confidence throughout 1905, but they were not confident enough to carry on struggling for their own demands. Many looked to the bourgeois feminists—confident, educated women—for a lead and had been attending the meetings of the Union of Women's Equality throughout the revolution. Kollontai went with them, noting that, "Working women who had begun to sense their inferior political status in terms of their sex were not ready to connect this with the general struggle of their class. They had yet to find the path that would lead them to their liberation, and still clung to the skirts of the bourgeois feminists" (Quoted in Porter, p96)

Kollontai observed the difficulties of bourgeois women and working class women organising together: "They tried to construct an idyllic, mixed union of grand-lady employers and domestic servants... They strove to organise domestic servants under the vigilant eyes of their mistresses" (Quoted in Tony Cliff, Alexandra Kollontai: Russian Marxists and Women Workers, 1981, www.marxists.org).

For instance, a cook began to organise meetings in her kitchen. Her mistress, a bourgeois feminist organiser, was supportive and often spoke at the meetings. However, when attendance at the meetings grew, the workers were never invited into the main house and had to stay stifled in the servants' quarters.

Kollontai and a group of socialist women around her organised a club for working class women, which would address their needs, including time off work for breast-feeding, workplace hygiene and pre- and post-natal care. The club ran every evening, attracting hundreds of workers. The club did, however, experience resistance from some Bolsheviks, including Bolshevik women, who were concerned that focussed work around women might sow division between women and men workers.

If working class women were to be involved in the fight back, the domestic burdens they faced would have to be lifted—so the club had a crèche and a buffet, as well as a library and daily lectures on socialism.

But as the revolutionary energy of 1905 faded, so did the new women's movement. A period of reaction was rising and revolutionaries were being rounded up in the streets by the Tsar's police.

In the toxic political environment of 1908 the feminists attempted to reinvigorate the women's movement through a united women's conference, the First All-Russian Congress of Women. However, despite talk of unity, the bourgeois feminists were no longer so willing to tolerate revolutionaries raising their demands as part of the movement. They were happy to still have working class women "clinging to their skirts" but didn't want working class political leadership.

Kollontai saw the conference as an opportunity to mobilise working women into action, but also a forum where the feminists' true class alliances might be tested—or exposed. The conference was supported by the trade unions and the organising committee included women textile workers, typographers and confectioners. Up to 650 women workers took part in meetings to build for the conference, at which Kollontai and her comrades spoke about the need for women's liberation to be part of the class struggle for socialism.

The bourgeois women capitalised on the Tsar's crackdown, requesting that the police keep Kollontai and the revolutionary women out of the conference. Nonetheless, they managed to attend, numbering 45 out of 1,053 delegates.

At the conference when bourgeois women spoke about sickness benefits, a woman worker shouted, "What do you know of our lives, bowling along in your carriages and splashing us in the mud?" (Porter, p139).

One bourgeois feminist argued that political parties should not be allowed in the women's movement. A Bolshevik woman pointed out that women of different classes had different demands and might need to organise in different ways. Membership of a working class party should be the right of working class women, as it was central to her struggle.

Kollontai spoke of the need for revolution:

"The woman question, say the feminists, is a question of 'rights and justice'. The woman question, answer the proletarian women, is a question of a 'piece of bread'... there is no independent woman question; the woman question arose as an integrated component of the social problem of our time. The liberation of woman as a member of society, a worker, an individual, a wife, and a mother, is possible therefore only together with the solution of the general social question, with the fundamental transformation of the present social order" (Quoted in Cliff).

In response, the bourgeois women unleashed fury on the working class delegates. Kollontai rushed out, only narrowly escaping arrest. The next day, twelve of the working class women were arrested at the conference. The political tension in the women's movement had indeed been revealed—for bourgeois women, equality within the system was the goal; for working class women this would never be enough.

Kollontai smuggled herself onto a train bound for Berlin. She would spend the next eight-and-a-half years in exile, mostly in Germany, only to return to Russia in the month following the revolutionary outburst of February 1917.

★ 6:
THE SOCIAL BASIS
OF THE WOMAN
QUESTION

Kollontai responded to the First All-Russian Congress of Women in her 1909 book The Social Basis of the Woman Question, in which she outlined a socialist approach to women's liberation. She asked, is a single united women's movement possible? She observed that, "The women's world is divided, just as is the world of men, into two camps; the interests and aspirations of one group of women bring it close to the bourgeois class, while the other group has close connections with the proletariat, and its claims for liberation encompass a full solution to the woman question."

There were circumstances where the women's movement could unite around certain demands, for example the right to vote, but, she argued, there was no escaping "that the feminists cannot, on account of their class position, fight for that fundamental transformation of the contemporary economic and social structure of society without which the liberation of women cannot be complete."

As Kollontai explained, "For the majority of women of the proletariat, equal rights with men would mean only an equal share in inequality, but for the 'chosen few', for the bourgeois women, it would indeed open doors to new and unprecedented rights and privileges that until now have been enjoyed by men of the bourgeois class alone."

These new privileges would give bourgeois women new weapons to exploit working class women with.

Kollontai also criticised the idea that men are responsible for women's oppression: "The feminists see men as the main enemy... Proletarian women have a different attitude. They do not see men as the enemy and the oppressor; on the contrary, they think of men as their comrades, who share with them the drudgery of the daily round and fight with them for a better future."

Kollontai drew on Engels's and Marx's understanding that the origin of women's oppression lay not in women's biology but in the rise of class societies, when private property and hierarchical family structures first appeared. The equality and cooperation that had characterised hunter-gatherer societies had meant that women's status was not defined by their ability to have children—nor were they burdened with all caring responsibilities, which were shared among members of the group. The emergence of a privileged class that was in a position to exploit others, and which owned and controlled the wealth, fundamentally transformed relations between people. Women were increasingly cut out of responsibility for production, losing the status that conferred, and given responsibility for all the caring duties related to the family.

The particular ways this happened varied from place to place and between different forms of class societies, but in all cases women found themselves pushed down the social hierarchy below their husbands, fathers and brothers.

Kollontai described how under capitalism, working women experienced a double burden—exploited at work, while also responsible for the majority of household work and child rearing. This provided capitalism with huge amounts of unpaid services. The development of the nuclear family—the father, mother and child unit—served to reinforce women's oppression. Women had no legal, financial or property rights separate from their husbands and no right to divorce them.

Middle class women did not face the same problems as working class women, as they could employ domestic servants and pay for a divorce. Kollontai discussed the bourgeois feminists demand for the "right to maternity" or the right to have a child out of wedlock. She argued that while this was an important demand, it was inadequate on its own. Rather than being a right to be fought for, "maternity has become the aim of a woman's life".

Kollontai recognised that the family and the home were also a source of immense comfort for people—"Blood and kinship ties at present often serve, it is true, as the only support in life, as the only refuge in times of hardship and misfortune." Her relationship with her son, Misha, was one of the most important in her life. But this source of comfort was also a source of oppression.

For Kollontai the liberation of women depended on the full socialisation of the work done in the home and complete political, educational and workplace equality for women. And this could only be achieved through a revolutionary struggle against capitalism and for socialism.

As for what would come next, "It is impossible to foretell what the relationships of the future, when the whole system has fundamentally been changed, will be like. But the slowly maturing evolution of relations between the sexes is clear evidence that ritual marriage and the compulsive isolated family are doomed to disappear."

★ 7: SEX AND THE STRUGGLE

In the spring of 1910 Kollontai was sent by the women of the St Petersburg textile workers' union to Copenhagen, Denmark, as a delegate to the Second International Socialist Women's Congress.

At the conference Clara Zetkin proposed 8 March as International Working Women's Day (IWWD) to unite the struggles of working women around the globe. Kollontai helped to organise the first IWWD demonstrations across Europe in 1911, with over a million marching in Germany, Austria, Denmark and Switzerland to demand the vote, equal pay and an end to workplace discrimination.

She described the energy and enthusiasm of the movement: "Halls were so packed that women had to ask the men to leave and give up their places to them. Husbands stayed at home with the children for a change, while their wives, the captive house-wives, went to meetings. Berlin was a seething sea of women" (Porter, p170).

In Russia IWWD was first celebrated in 1913 in St Petersburg, with a rally of 1,000 addressed by women from the textile workers' union.

Also in 1913, the Bolshevik party decided to print a special journal focusing specifically on women workers, Rabotnitsa (The Woman Worker). It was edited by leading Bolshevik women including Inessa Armand and Nadezhda

Krupskaya. Battling police censorship and relying on money collected from women workers, it dealt with issues including maternity leave, childcare, working conditions, health issues, the family and electoral issues. Some women Bolsheviks opposed the Rabotnista, concerned that it might sow divisions between women and men.

The outbreak of the First World War signalled the end of the Rabotnitsa after only seven issues. It would be re-launched three years later, in the heat of revolution.

Kollontai also used her time in exile to explore the impact that capitalism has on people's sexual relationships. She described how women's oppression resulted in unequal and often fraught relations between men and women. Kollontai drew on own experiences, both her early marriage and the relationships she went on to have, including with Bolshevik organiser Alexander Shlyapnikov and later the Bolshevik sailor, Pavel Dybenko, who was 17 years her junior.

While relationships occupied an important part of Kollontai's life, they also frustrated her. The all-consuming nature of love promoted by bourgeois society clashed with her desire to write and work for the revolution. Despite loving him, she would often express relief that after a lengthy visit from Shlyapnikov, she could finally focus on her work.

She expressed this frustration in one of short stories: "I've read enough novels to know just how much time and energy it takes to fall in love and I just don't have time..."

Her personal life did not go without comment. The right wing journalist Pitirim Sorokin wrote of Kollontai in 1917, "As for this woman, it is plain that her revolutionary enthusiasm is nothing but a gratification of her sexual satyriasis" (Holt, p29).

She also faced criticism when she wrote, "The sexual act must be seen not as something shameful and sinful but as something which is as natural as the other needs of healthy organism, such as hunger or thirst" (Holt, p229). Some Bolsheviks felt her ideas were too in advance of the majority of workers, others that they would distract young workers from the revolutionary struggle.

Yet Kollontai was not alone in her desire to challenge the ideal of romantic love. Women entering the workplace, living in cities away from the restrictions of rural life, was changing relationships. In "The New Woman" (1918) Kollontai examined how this was reflected in literature. Kollontai quotes Agnes, a working class Russian heroine:

"Why all this for only one person?... If one must forget oneself, then I would rather do it not just for one person alone, by preparing a good noon meal and a restful slumber for him; if such be the case I will grant all that also to such-and-such other unhappy ones..."

Kollontai felt that romantic love occupied far too high a place in society: "You probably won't find a time when the problems of sex have occupied such a central place in the life of society...sexual dramas have served as such a never-ending source of inspiration for every sort of art" (Sexual Relations and the Class Struggle, 1921).

Kollontai developed her ideas in an essay, "Sexual Relations and the Class Struggle", which she wrote while in exile and which was published in 1921 by the Bolshevik government. She argued that, "Sexuality and sexual relationships were an essential part of what it means to be human. However, under capitalism, relationships were based on strict individualism and exclusiveness which is located in the institution of the private nuclear family. Women's domestic work further structured inequality into relationships. Kollontai described how this created immense pressure on individuals and "unavoidable loneliness of spirit".

"Man experiences this 'loneliness' even in towns full of shouting, noise and people, even in a crowd of close friends and work-mates. Because of their loneliness men are apt to cling in a predatory and unhealthy way to illusions about finding a 'soul mate' from among the members of the opposite sex."

This can lead people to take out their feelings of insecurity and loneliness on their loved ones. "To be rid of the eternally present threat of loneliness, we 'launch an attack' on the emotions of the person we love with a cruelty and lack of delicacy that will not be understood by future generations."

Further, the ideal of "one true love" encourages people to act as though they own their partners. "Bourgeois morality, with its introverted individualistic family based entirely on private property, has carefully cultivated the idea that one partner should completely 'possess' the other... We demand the right to know every secret of this person's being...We are unable to follow the simplest rule of love—that another person should be treated with great consideration."

Kollontai asked what the solution to bourgeois love might be. She pointed out that working class communities had always experimented with different types of relationships, whether through affairs, having children out of wedlock or same-sex relationships. Middle class people were also experimenting with living together without marrying—sometimes called "free marriage"—and with group relationships.

But even in experimental relationships, women were still subject to double standards. Men had a certain freedom to act without moral judgement from society; women did not. So Kollontai was scathing of those middle class proponents of "free marriage" or "free love" (having sexual relationships without the ties of marriage or partnership) in the here and now who didn't recognise the inequalities of class and gender.

In a society based on exploitation and oppression, "free marriage" and "free love" could in practice simply mean women with children abandoned by men with no responsibility to support them. This didn't mean that new kinds of relationships couldn't or shouldn't be fought for, but that this struggle could not be separated from the wider fight for a world based on equality, cooperation and human needs—a communist society. It was in being part of collective struggles that men and women could begin to break down the hypocritical and oppressive morals of capitalist society and strive to create new kinds of relationships.

Only then, Kollontai argued, could you begin to talk about a genuine "free love". Only when the material needs of all people were met socially could all individuals—and women in particular—freely choose whether to enter into or leave a relationship: "No more domestic bondage for women. No more inequality within the family. No need for women to fear being left without support and with children to bring up. The woman in communist society no longer depends upon her husband."

★ 8: NO TO WAR

Throughout Kollontai's time in exile, the tensions between the dominant countries of Europe were growing and war was looming.

Some socialists, including Kollontai, saw the threat of war and actively opposed it. They recognised that the ramping up of jingoistic nationalism was simply a cover for the economic competition between the imperial powers—France, Britain, Russia, Germany and so on—spilling over into political and military competition to divide up the rest of the world between them. A world war would mean millions of workers being sent to kill each other in the interests of profit.

Other socialists, such as many of the leaders of the German SPD, spoke out against war and signed pledges to oppose it, but denied that war was possible. They believed that the ruling classes of the different competing nation states had a common interest in maintaining the stability of capitalism and that it was not in their interest to go to war with each other.

Kollontai worked hard to build the movement against the threat of war. She became closer politically to the Bolsheviks, who consistently campaigned against war, unlike the Mensheviks.

When war broke out in August 1914, most of the leaders

of Europe's socialist movements and trade unions, including the German SPD, supported their own governments. The Bolsheviks and the Serbian socialists were the only major socialist parties to openly oppose the war. Across the globe groups of bourgeois feminists dropped their campaigns for the vote and supported the war, while trade union leaders lined up behind their governments and actively opposed strikes by their own members.

Nearly 28 million people would lose their lives in the blood bath of the First World War. By the end of the first year, Russia alone had suffered nearly a million deaths.

Kollontai at first aligned herself with the pacifists who opposed all forms of war. In contrast, the Bolsheviks, led by Lenin, argued for the imperialist war to be turned into a revolutionary civil war of workers, soldiers and peasants against their own ruling classes.

But as the war went on, it became increasingly clear to Kollontai that the only way to the end it was through the workers and peasants turning against their own ruling class. The calls by the Mensheviks for "peace" sounded hollow against a backdrop of poverty and bloodshed.

Kollontai re-joined the Bolshevik party in 1915 and helped to establish a new international organisation of anti-war revolutionaries alongside German socialists such as Rosa Luxemburg and Karl Liebknecht.

That same year she accepted an invitation by German socialists in the United States to take part in a four-month-long tour, speaking to workers about why they should oppose the war.

Her journey took her from New York to San Francisco, speaking in over 100 towns, to thousands of workers, in Russian, German and English. She addressed a group of workers mourning the murder of the Industrial Workers of the World (IWW) organiser and songwriter, Joe Hill. She met the leader of the IWW, Bill Haywood, and spoke alongside the prominent socialist and five-time presidential candidate, Eugene V Debs.

In the summer of 1915 the Russian army suffered enormous defeats on the Eastern Front. Industry and transport were in near collapse and there was hardly any food. Riots spread across the cities.

Lenin encouraged Kollontai to write a pamphlet, Who Needs War? which was published in millions of copies, in several languages and distributed to troops.

She wrote, "In order to achieve peace, the first thing to be done is to bring the culprits to book. And who are the culprits if not the Tsars and Kaisers... My enemy is in my own country, and this enemy is the same for all the workers of the world. The enemy is capitalism, this enemy is the rapacious, corrupt class government..." (Who Needs War?, 1915).

As 1917 approached, Kollontai returned to exile in Norway. The war was deepening, millions more dying. At the same time, strikes and protests were on the rise in Russia.

★ 9: THE REVOLUTION BEGINS

'**W**e, the women workers, were the first to raise the Red Banner in the days of the Russian Revolution, the first to go out onto the streets on Women's Day" (Kollontai, Our Tasks, 1917).

The revolution that broke out on International Working Women's Day 1917—23 February by the Russian calendar—was ignited by the working class women of Petrograd (as St Petersburg had been renamed in 1914, to remove any hint of Germanness). These women had been described in January 1917 by a Tsarist official as a "store of combustible material".

Fuelled by anger at three years of brutal war and famine, women textile workers in Petrograd went on strike. They marched past the main factories, calling out the male workers.

A Petrograd worker from the Nobel engineering factory recalled, "Masses of women workers in a militant frame of mind filled the lane. Those who caught sight of us began to wave their arms, shouting, 'Come out!' 'Stop work!' Snowballs flew through the windows. We decided to join the revolution" (Quoted in Harman, A People's History of the World, Verso, 2009, p413).

The next day workers in the massive Putilov arms factory were locked out of work. They marched into the streets, where housewives and women workers joined them. Their banners read, "Down with war! Down with high prices! Down with hunger! Bread for the workers!" (Hillyar and McDermid, p147).

When the Tsar's police used whips to try to disperse the protesters, women workers responded by spreading the strike. By the second day over 150,000 workers from more than 130 factories were on strike, demanding the fall of the Tsar and an end to the war. Soldiers mutinied and refused to fire on protesters.

As in 1905, women workers proved themselves to be the most bold and courageous. Many of them were the wives of soldiers, and they invaded soldiers' bunkers and demanded they put down their guns and join the strike. Soon 167,000 soldiers had mutinied, students had joined the protests and there was a general strike in Petrograd. The strike spread across the country, from Petrograd to Moscow, to smaller cities and villages in the East where peasants were seizing control of the land.

Bolshevik women were at the heart of the resistance. The Bolshevik metalworker Nina Agadzhanova led demonstrations of tram and metalworkers and freed political prisoners from jails and barracks. The student Bolshevik Alexandra Singer ran the telephone exchange when the majority of workers deserted.

Red Guards (armed groups of workers) were organised to monitor the streets. The soviets, or mass workers' councils, that had formed during the 1905 revolution, were swiftly re-organised. The Petrograd Soviet consisted of delegates from factories and regiments across the capital. Within days, Tsar Nicholas II had fallen.

The workers in the soviets did not yet have the

confidence to seize power for themselves. After the fall of the Tsar, there was a period of "dual power" in which both a Provisional Government and the Soviets ruled Russia. The Provisional Government was made up of representatives of the capitalist class, such as Alexander Kerensky. The soviets were comprised of delegates elected by the workers, soldiers and peasants. The Provisional Government supported the continuation of war, against the wishes of most workers. It delayed elections in order to avoid the question.

As soon as she read the headline "Revolution in Russia", Kollontai made urgent plans to return to Russia. Lenin, who was also still in exile in Switzerland, convinced her to hold back a week in order to receive his "Letters from Afar". In his telegram to her, he warned revolutionary workers from forming alliances with the liberal, capitalist class: "Our tactics—absolute distrust of the Provisional Government" (Porter, p230).

Kollontai boarded a train headed for Russia, Lenin's "Letters from Afar" hidden in her corset. On arrival in Finland she boarded a sledge, and as she hastened towards Russia she recalled feeling elated despite the freezing cold. "Ahead was struggle and work, work and struggle. On that day, my soul felt bracingly bright and fresh as the snow and the frosty air around us" (Porter, p232).

At the border, the Tsar's longstanding warrant for her arrest was torn up by officials and the train drivers explained to her, "The people are the bosses now! You're not just a worker, you're a citizen" (Porter, p231).

Kollontai found Petrograd transformed by protests and demonstrations. She joined a street protest by soldiers and soldiers' widows and wives, the "soldatki". The soldiers lifted her onto their shoulders as they yelled, "Bread for our children!" and "Down with war!" (Porter, p237). She could see that, despite the achievements so far, the revolution had much further to go.

Kollontai was at odds with the leadership of the Bolsheviks in Russia, including Stalin and Kamenev, the editors of the party newspaper, Pravda. They believed that the revolution in Russia must stop at a bourgeois revolution, like the French or English revolutions. Capitalism needed to fully develop in Russia before the working class would be ready for socialism.

Kollontai, guided by Lenin's "Letters from Afar", disagreed. She felt the revolution must continue. This was the only way Russian workers could bring the war to an end and begin the fight for real liberation.

Under the Provisional Government the cost of living sky-rocketed. There was lack of food, peasants were still bound to the land owners and more soldiers were dying on the front. The liberal middle classes were committed to keeping Russia in the war, and ensuring that the working class and peasantry paid the price.

Kollontai wrote in Pravda in March, "Today sees the completion of the first stage of the revolution, the stage which consists of the destruction of the old. Now, comrades, let us hasten back to work!... We must build a new, democratic, free Russia!" ("Our Memorial to the Fighters for Freedom", 1917).

Kollontai's arguments resonated with workers, and she was made a delegate of the Petrograd Soviet.

On 3 April Lenin finally returned to Russia. Kollontai and several other comrades, along with huge numbers of workers, soldiers and sailors, travelled to greet him at the Finnish border. In his speech, however, he immediately began a row with the leadership of the Bolsheviks, declaring that the revolution against the Tsar must be turned into a workers' revolution against the Provisional Government.

The following day, when Lenin addressed a party meeting, Kollontai was alone in getting up to speak in defence of his position. She was described unflatteringly in Pravda as the "Valkyrie of the Revolution"—the chooser of the dead (Porter, p244).

Throughout the spring, Lenin and his supporters, including Kollontai, waged a sharp debate within the party for accelerating the revolution. The strikes and protests continued to increase and ideas and positions sharpened. Within three weeks, the majority of the Bolsheviks voted for Lenin's position.

Now, the pressing task for the Bolsheviks was to win the majority of the working class and the soviets to their position. They did this through involvement in the strikes and demonstrations and patiently explaining the need to spread the revolution, overthrow the Provisional Government and end the war.

★10: WOMEN WORKERS LEAD THE WAY

With so many men away at war, women now made up 43 percent of workers in Petrograd. In some workplaces they outnumbered men. Women workers were central to the strikes in the spring of 1917. One strike involving the unions of maids, restaurant workers and chocolate factory workers, won a demand for a 125 percent increase in pay for women and a 100 percent increase for men.

Kollontai helped to organise the 40,000 laundresses who went on strike in May over pay and conditions. The Bolshevik laundress, Goncharova, helped to raise the women's confidence by going from one laundry to the next, winning more women to the strike, filling buckets with ice cold water to put out the ovens. When an owner of one of the laundries tried to attack Goncharova with a crowbar, the women responded by grabbing him from behind and chucking him out.

Kollontai spent much of May campaigning against the war among sailors in the Baltic Sea fleet in Helsingfors, Finland. Thousands of the sailors had read her anti-war pamphlet and were joining the Bolsheviks in droves. In response, the Provisional Government tried to dissolve the fleet. It was here that Kollontai met the Bolshevik sailor Pavel Dybenko. He was a veteran of a naval mutiny in 1915 and had been imprisoned for his anti-war activities. Together they addressed mass meetings of sailors, arguing for the revolution to continue.

Back in Russia, Kollontai was involved in the relaunch of the Bolshevik women's newspaper, Rabotnitsa. Even where women workers were a majority, the legacy of years of oppression meant that men were the majority in the leadership bodies of the revolution—the soviets. In Moscow, where over half of factory workers were women, they made up only 259 out of 4,743 delegates in May 1917.

If the revolution was to succeed, women, and their demands, must be raised. Kollontai, in an article in Pravda on 5 May, criticised the agenda of the coming trade union congress for not including a discussion of equal pay for women.

By May 1917 Rabotnitsa had a circulation of 40-50,000. Rabotnitsa exposed the bosses and the rich as responsible for women's inequality in the workplace, and argued that it was in male workers' interests to fight for women's rights.

Kollontai spoke to a trade union congress on 21 June: "The class-conscious worker must understand the value of female labour and that, by threatening to replace male labour with cheaper female workers, the capitalist can put pressure on men's wages" (Quoted in Petty, Roberts and Smith, Women's Liberation and Socialism, Bookmarks, 1987, p40).

Kollontai wrote in Rabotnitsa, "the success of the workers' struggle for a better life...now depends not only on the consciousness and organisation of the men, but also on the number of women workers entering the ranks of the organised working class" ("Our Tasks", 1917).

★11: A SUMMER OF RESISTANCE

The summer of 1917 was tumultuous. There was widespread famine and impoverishment, fuelling fury at the war.

In early June Kollontai was sent back to Helsingfors to win the support of Finnish comrades for the revolution to continue.

Later in June, in a desperate attempt to restore national unity, leader of the Provisional Government Kerensky launched a renewed military offensive. The offensive was a disaster, and things got worse for Kerensky when the press exposed a secret note from his foreign secretary Miliukov promising the Allied powers that Russia would continue to fight the war.

From 2 to 7 July there were mass demonstrations, strikes and riots by angry soldiers and workers in Petrograd, demanding the immediate downfall of the Provisional Government.

Kollontai, who was at a conference in Sweden during what became known as the July Days, saw the actions of the workers, soldiers and sailors as proof that the working class was moving towards revolution.

The Bolsheviks supported the resistance of workers, sailors and soldiers, while arguing for them to hold back from insurrection until the majority of the working class and the peasantry were convinced that the soviets should take power. A premature uprising could leave the most militant sections of the working class isolated and vulnerable to attack from the Provisional Government.

In response to the July Days, Kerensky led a witch-hunt against revolutionaries. Workers' newspapers were banned, the death penalty for soldiers was reinstated and Bolsheviks were rounded up and imprisoned. The government whipped up hatred and fear against revolutionaries.

Lenin was labelled a "German spy" and was forced into hiding in Finland. Most of the leadership of the Bolsheviks was either imprisoned or in hiding. The witch-hunt had a profound effect on the working class. Lenin and the Bolsheviks were damaged in the eyes of the masses. Members tore up their membership cards.

But many Bolsheviks also defended the party, like the group of women workers who cleaned the editorial office of Rabotnitsa before the police raided it. They distributed all the remaining papers to workers in the factories at night.

On her return from Sweden, a warrant was issued for Kollontai's arrest. The waiter on the train refused to serve her, calling her a "bloodthirsty bitch". After crossing the border she was arrested and imprisoned for almost two months. It could not have been more different from the warm reception she had received on her return just five months earlier.

From prison, Kollontai retained her revolutionary optimism. "The Provisional Government can't respond to people's needs for an end to the war, land to the peasants, and power to the workers, it's merely marking time. It doesn't understand that history demands a step forward to a new, socialist future!" (Porter, p258).

In August the Tsarist General Kornilov attempted to lead a military coup. At first Kerensky manoeuvred to support him, believing Kornilov would limit his attack to the Bolsheviks. However, Kornilov was after Kerensky as well, and overnight Kerensky swapped positions.

The Bolsheviks argued for workers to form a temporary united front with Kerensky and the Provisional Government, to defend the revolution against the military coup. Railway workers and soldiers prevented troops being moved to join the regiments being sent by Kornilov to attack Petrograd. Women workers built barricades and organised medical aid.

The defeat of the Kornilov coup convinced the majority of workers and soldiers that the Bolsheviks were the only party genuinely on their side. Kerensky's opportunism was exposed. The Bolsheviks won a majority in the soviets, with Trotsky, who had joined the party, at the head of the Petrograd Soviet, as he had been in 1905.

On her release from prison Kollontai learned that her commitment to the revolution and opposing the war had secured her a place on the Bolshevik central committee.

★12: INSURRECTION

The protests, strikes and peasant uprisings continued into the autumn. The confidence and willingness to fight of the class convinced the soviets that the time had come to take power from the Provisional Government. The majority of the All Russian Congress of Soviets voted to back an insurrection.

In late October huge strikes swept from the capital across the country. Red Guards came onto the streets and Kerensky's government locked themselves into the Winter Palace. Bolsheviks could no longer hold back from revolution.

On 25 October, the Red Guard entered the Winter Palace and arrested the government.

That night at a mass meeting at the Smolny Institute, headquarters of the Petrograd Soviet, crowds roared with applause when Lenin spoke: "We shall now proceed to the construction of the socialist order."

In his account of the revolution, the American journalist John Reed described how, "A grizzled soldier sobbed openly and Alexandra Kollontai rapidly blinked back the tears as the immense sound rolled through the hall, burst out the windows and doors and soared into the quiet sky" (Ten Days That Shook the World, Penguin, 1966, p133).

Kollontai wrote, "If I were asked what was the greatest, the most memorable moment of my life, I would answer without any hesitation: it was when Soviet power was proclaimed... 'All power has passed to the Soviets of Workers', Soldiers' and Peasants' Deputies!'" (Lenin at Smolny, 1971).

In the days following the insurrection, workers, soldiers and peasants threw themselves into defence of the revolution. Many lost their lives. Slutskaya, who had worked with Kollontai on Rabotnitsa, was killed delivering aid across a barricade.

Revolutions are about self-emancipation. They are not single-day events, or straightforward processes; they can take months or even years. They are not achieved by the actions of great leaders; they come from the self-organisation of the most oppressed and exploited in society. This was nowhere more true than in Russia in 1917.

The October Revolution is the single example of a genuine socialist revolution in which the working class took power and began to run things for themselves. Marx had envisioned how through the process of revolution the working class would become capable of ridding itself of all the "muck of ages"—of all the sexism, racism and bigotry in society—and become "fitted to found society anew".

In the weeks and months following the October Revolution there was a flourishing of discussion and debate. It was a "festival of the oppressed". Some 125,000 schools for literacy were formed, public squares were filled to bursting with workers and peasants watching theatre and poetry.

The Bolsheviks also set up state schools, ensuring that there was free education for all. All private institutions were abolished, so even children of aristocrats attended state schools. The schools drew on and developed some of the most advanced pedagogical practices in the world.

The revolution signalled a huge shift in the way the Bolsheviks organised. They went from being agitators putting demands on the Provisional Government, to writing decrees and issuing laws themselves. They overturned all the reactionary Tsarist and capitalist laws and institutions. All oppressed nation states and religious minorities were granted complete freedom. In a matter of days, the Russian state went from being one of the most reactionary in the world, to the most progressive.

The revolution extended to Muslims in the eastern parts of the former Russian Empire. In April 1917 there had been the first All-Russian Muslim Women's Congress that adopted resolutions in support of political equality between women and men, including divorce rights. After October, there was the First All-Russian Congress of Muslims, which called for equal rights for women, and opposition to purdah (screening women from the view of men) and polygamy. The Muslim communities in Russia were the first in the world to liberate women from the institutions that were common practice for Islamic societies of the time.

In November 1917 Kollontai and other leading Bolshevik women organised a Peasant and Working Women's Congress. On the day, they waited to greet the 80 delegates they expected. They were overwhelmed by over 500 delegates, many with their hair in scarves and carrying their children. They represented around 80,000 women workers, trade unionists and peasants.

The policies that Kollontai and others would go on to implement, and the changes they brought for women, were among the finest achievements of the revolution.

★13: COMMISSAR OF SOCIAL WELFARE

The Commissariat of Social Welfare was responsible for the care of children, mothers, elderly people and disabled people. Kollontai headed the department, replacing the liberal Countess Panina, who had been Minister of Welfare and Education in the Provisional Government and who expressed horror at Kollontai's politics. "This absurd Madame Kollontai invites the servants to come and sit in armchairs at her meetings. Such things cannot be!" (Quoted in Louise Bryant, Six Months in Russia, 1918).

Kollontai made all workers in the department equal. She recalled, "We were hungry, we rarely succeeded in getting a night's sleep, there were so many difficulties and dangers, but we all worked passionately, for we were in a hurry to build the new Soviet life, and felt that everything we did today was desperately needed tomorrow, however rough and ready" (Porter, p272).

Louise Bryant, a radical journalist from the US, spent time with Kollontai during this period. Bryant made frequent visits to Kollontai's office and described how remarkable it was to see former servants playing a leading role. She recalled that every day there would be a line of "sweet-faced old people" outside Kollontai's offices. Kollontai explained that she had removed the managers of the old people's homes and had made them into mini-republics. The residents elected their own officers, debated priorities and chose their menus. They visited her offices daily to express thanks.

Bryant asked how much say they could really have over their menus when faced with food shortages on a national scale. Kollontai laughed, "Surely...you must understand that there is a great deal of moral satisfaction in deciding whether you want thick cabbage soup or thin cabbage soup!" (Quoted in Bryant)

In her role as Commissar of Social Welfare Kollontai helped to write the groundbreaking decrees that opened the way for liberation. Hereditary laws were abolished, as was the authority of men in the family. Divorce was legalised and the distinction between "legitimate" and "illegitimate" children was removed. Marriage ceremonies were simplified so any man of 18 and woman of 16 could marry through a short civil ceremony. Kollontai and Dybenko were the first couple married under the new law.

Kollontai also helped to assemble a six-person team that looked at the conditions for mothers at work. Their first decree demanded free crèches at work and time off to breastfeed. Women were given four months maternity leave, far in advance of any other country in the world at the time.

Equal pay between men and women was introduced, and all workplace conditions were equalised. The eight-hour day was established. Women and young people were prohibited from night work, heavy or dangerous production, or working underground.

The Bolsheviks knew decrees alone were not enough. Women's domestic burden must be lifted. Kollontai helped to set up communal nurseries, restaurants, hostels, laundries and schools, which began to free worker and peasant women from their household drudgery.

Prostitution, which had been widespread under the Tsar, almost disappeared. The rich men who paid for prostitutes had largely fled during the revolution. Women who did turn to prostitution were seen as victims of economic circumstances and sexism, not as criminals.

Kollontai sought to make communal childcare and maternity centres a reality. The first state run maternity hospital and mother and baby home had a library, a medical laboratory and its own dairy.

Supporters of the old Tsarist regime spread rumours that the Bolsheviks were forcing women to separate from their children. Kollontai rejected these accusations. Tsarist Russia had neglected and let the children of working class women starve. The socialist state ensured that every child had a carer, but parents were never forced to use communal services.

The efforts of the Commissariat of Social Welfare were hampered by supporters of the old regime, as well as by the poverty Russia was facing due to war. On the eve of the opening of the first women and children's home, Kollontai received word that it had been set on fire by anti-revolution forces.

Though the revolution had won and the work of building a new society had begun, the revolution's enemies had not disappeared. The Tsar's supporters were regrouping and getting organised to launch a counter-revolution, which would grow into a civil war, ravaging Russia for the next two years.

★14: CIVIL WAR

The Tsar's supporters were organised in what became known as the White Armies. These forces were armed to the hilt by 14 foreign states, including Germany, Britain, Japan, the United States and France. The Great Powers of Europe and beyond recognised that workers' revolution in Russia was a threat to all of them—especially if it inspired war-weary soldiers and workers elsewhere to rise up against their own rulers.

Almost immediately after the revolution, the Great Powers imposed an economic blockade on the new workers' state in Russia, exacerbating an already dire situation. Workers and peasants who had withstood almost four years of war and hunger, were now attempting to build a new society in those same terrible conditions.

An urgent task for the Bolshevik government was to end Russia's participation in the war. They did this on 3 March 1918 by signing the Treaty of Brest-Litovsk with the Central Powers (German Empire, Austria-Hungary, Bulgaria and the Ottoman Empire).

Kollontai opposed the Bolsheviks' acceptance of the treaty. She felt it abandoned countries like Finland and Ukraine to the imperialist warmongers and that the new socialist state should be prepared to fight a "revolutionary war" against Germany.

Brest-Litovsk was certainly a compromise with the imperialist countries, but Lenin and Trotsky believed they had no choice but to accept it. The White Armies were attacking and the Red Army of the workers' state could not fight them off if they were still engaged in the war.

Russia could not fight a revolutionary war against the German Empire—it would take revolutions by the working classes of neighbouring countries for the leaders to topple. And if revolution didn't spread, the Russian Revolution would not survive.

Due to her disagreements over Brest-Litovsk, Kollontai resigned from her position as Commissar of Social Welfare. Still, she agreed with Lenin and Trotksy that the revolution must spread.

The Bolsheviks were forced to take a series of harsh measures to address the threat of starvation in the cities. The population of Petrograd alone had fallen from 2.4 million in 1917 to 574,000 in August 1920, with many having died of disease or starvation and others fleeing to the countryside in search of food. The government implemented a policy known as War Communism. Grain was seized from peasants to feed the Red Army and workers in the cities, and strict controls and rationing were put in place to try to stem the black market. This put huge strains on the relationship between workers and peasants, encouraging some right wing peasant organisations to side with the White Army over the Bolsheviks.

As many as 73,858 women fought for the Bolsheviks, and nearly 2,000 lost their lives in the civil war, which raged until 1920. Kollontai organised women in political work, spending most of the spring and summer of 1918 travelling the country on "agit-trains" and steamers. Using films, slide shows, pamphlets and speeches, they rallied the Red Army and people across Russia to defend the revolution.

★ 15: THE COMMUNIST WOMAN

While the revolution had delivered huge gains for women on paper, the economic blockade and the ravages of the civil war period meant that women were still experiencing oppression in practice. In response, the Bolsheviks committed themselves to focussed work among women.

Lenin welcomed Kollontai back into party work and a second Congress for Worker and Peasant Women was organised for November of 1918. Some 1,147 working class and peasant women crammed into a hall meant for 300.

The mood in the room was defiant. Armand spoke about the need for communal nurseries, which was answered by calls of "We won't give up our children!" (Porter, p304). Rising to speak, Kollontai reassured them that state schools would guarantee universal childcare and education, but not force women to separate from their children.

She also recognised that while progressive divorce laws were helping those in unhappy relationships, they were also frightening to women, especially those who still relied on their husbands financially.

She explained how the socialist state was beginning the process of setting up communal services that could lift women's work in the home:

"Special clothes-mending centres will free the working

woman from the hours spent on mending and give her the opportunity to devote her evenings to reading, attending meetings and concerts" (Communism and the Family, 1920).

Lenin spoke at the congress to affirm the state's commitment to abolish all restrictions on women's rights. His and Kollontai's words were received with enthusiasm, delegates burst into singing the "Internationale".

The congress passed special proposals on provision for mothers and young children, and laid the foundation for methodical work throughout the country aimed at the liberation of women. Kollontai and a handful of other Bolshevik women were elected to form a new Women's Commission under Armand. Each branch of the party would have a local women's commission attached to it.

Now the real work began. Communal canteens were vital to lifting the burden on individual households, and by 1920 60 percent of Moscow citizens were registered at communal canteens and 90 percent were registered in Petrograd. Some 300,000 families were relocated out of the slums into communal flats in mansions previously belonging to the rich. These were still far from ideal. People were sharing cramped rooms with strangers.

In January 1919, exhausted and overworked, Kollontai suffered a heart attack and was bedridden for three months. After she had recovered she was sent to do agitational work on the Southern Front in Ukraine, where White Army forces were gathering.

She returned to Petrograd in the summer of 1919. She found that the Women's Commission had become the Zhenotdel (women's department). It had a newspaper, Communist Woman, which was its main organisational tool. It acted in the interests of women and had legal powers to protect women's rights at work and in the home. It had a delegate-based apprenticeship programme, in order to train women in political leadership, organisational tasks and administration.

Kollontai was in charge of work with the peasantry. She helped ensure that every province of European Russia had a Zhenotdel. She also organised delegations of Bolshevik women, often wearing headscarves or veils, to the east to work with Muslim women, running educational programmes and promoting political activity.

The religious freedom won through the revolution meant that there were significant advances for oppressed religious groups. There was a Muslim Commissariat in Moscow, which looked after the interests of Muslims. A majority of Muslim leaders supported the workers' state. A number of Muslim women were also recruited into party work.

Ill health due to typhus and a weak heart meant Kollontai's activity was interrupted continually through 1919 and 1920. It wasn't until the autumn of 1920, following Armand's death from cholera, that Kollontai returned as organiser of the Zhenotdel.

She set about reviving the Commission on Women's Sexual Health, which was a matter of urgency. The disruption of the civil war had seen a spike in sexually transmitted diseases, post-natal complications and dangerous abortions. The legalisation of abortion in 1920 made strides towards tackling these issues.

Kollontai maintained her active commitment to the Zhenotdel, even as economic collapse at the end of the civil war in 1920 made it almost impossible to deliver the communal provisions women needed.

★ 16: THE WORKERS' OPPOSITION

By the spring of 1920, the Red Army had beaten back the White Armies and successfully defended revolutionary Russia. However, they paid a huge price for the victory. Russia was politically isolated and surrounded by hostile imperialist states. The country was facing famine, disease and economic crisis. Production was at a fifth of pre-war levels.

The policy of War Communism had unleashed fury and rebellion among sections of the peasantry, presenting a very real threat to the revolution. Numbers of former Tsarist officials had been brought back into positions of power in order to save the state from collapse. There was a growing bureaucracy in the government and the party.

Many of the workers who had fought hardest during the revolution had died defending it in the civil war. People who had only months before been peasants were now working in the factories or as sailors. They had little experience of trade union organisation or socialist ideas, and they rebelled against the workers' state.

This sparked a heated debate within the Bolshevik party about how they should relate to this new working class. Kollontai joined a group within the party called the Workers' Opposition, led by prominent trade unionists. She wrote an important article outlining its aims. They argued that the trade unions—rather than the state—should take complete control of production in order to return to the ideal of workers' control and counteract the tendency towards bureaucratic rule.

But this ignored the perilous state of Russia. At the congress, Trotsky argued that the immediate dangers to the revolution meant that the state should control the unions to stop the peasants' counter-revolution. Lenin and the majority of the party leaders argued for a balance where the trade unions would be allowed to defend the interests of workers, while the state and the party would control industry in the interests of society as a whole.

The extremely high stakes in this debate were shown by the revolt of sailors at the Kronstadt Fortress near Petrograd, which coincided with the Tenth Party Congress. The uprising presented a real danger to the new government. The bloody suppression of the uprising revealed how difficult the choices had become for the Bolsheviks.

In response to these pressures, the Bolsheviks relaxed the policy of War Communism and introduced the New Economic Policy (NEP) in 1921. This put in place some financial incentives to peasants to produce grain. Lenin saw the NEP as a temporary and necessary evil to stop the peasantry leading a counter-revolution.

After months of the Workers' Opposition operating openly and using the party's press, the Congress voted to temporarily ban factions. Kollontai made a speech calling for the Workers' Opposition to break from the party.

Weeks later, at the Eleventh Party Congress, Kollontai faced expulsion for her involvement in the faction. A majority of delegates voted against expelling her, but she was severely censured. She had already been removed from her position in the Zhenotdel in early February.

★ 17:
THE RISE
OF STALIN

Joseph Stalin had been a member of the Bolshevik Party from its formation in 1903. He had been on the central committee of the party throughout 1917, though he never played a leading role on the scale of Lenin or Trotsky. After the civil war, Stalin began to form a faction within the party based on the bureaucracy.

It was the growing bureaucracy that selected Stalin as general secretary in 1922 and leader in 1923. He turned the party machine into a body completely faithful to him, retreating from the radicalism of the early years of the revolution and abandoning Lenin and Trotsky's vision of international revolution.

The growth of the bureaucracy was a product of the desperate need to hold on to power in a country devastated by war and isolated by the failure of revolution to spread to other nations. Lenin warned of the dangers of the growing bureaucracy and how it was distorting the party and the revolution. From his sick bed in December 1922, he argued that Stalin must be removed as general secretary. Lenin died in January 1924. From then on, Stalin officially took the position of leader of the Soviet Union.

The only thing that could have saved the Russian Revolution was revolution in other, especially European, countries. But Stalin's bureaucracy opposed the call for international revolution. He refused Trotsky's proposal that they travel to Germany to support the revolution there and he cautioned the German Communists against challenging for power at a pivotal moment in their uprising. This intervention ultimately helped crush the German Revolution, which could have been crucial to saving Russia.

"Socialism in one country" acted as a slogan for Stalin and his followers to unite around. Stalin painted internationalists like Trotsky as "unpatriotic".

In late 1922, while in Odessa, Kollontai received a call from Stalin relocating her to Norway. Her removal from Russia was a convenient way of ending her involvement in the party's activities—a form of political exile. She would remain an overseas ambassador for the Soviet Union for the rest of her life.

Kollontai's decision to accept the position is perhaps a reflection of the isolation and retreat of revolutionary Russia. But it meant that she withdrew from the struggle to preserve the gains that women had achieved at a time when Stalin began systematically wiping them out.

Trotsky formed a group, the Left Opposition, to continue the fight against the rise of Stalin's bureaucracy, arguing for revolutionaries in Russia to build workers' democracy and solidarity with international workers' struggles. Kollontai engaged with Trotsky's Left Opposition when she briefly returned to Moscow in 1927, but she refused to give him political support, stressing the need for "party unity".

Shlyapnikov was outraged that Kollontai was not on Trotsky's side. When he called her a "careerist" she rejected this, claiming that Trotksy's position was "deeply alien" to her (Beatrice Farnsworth, "Conversing with Stalin, Surviving the Terror: The Diaries of Aleksandra Kollontai and the Internal Life of Politics", Slavic Review, 2010, p955).

In his autobiography, Trotsky observed that Kollontai

"waged many a battle against the Lenin-Trotsky regime, only to bow most movingly later on to the Stalin regime" (Trotsky, My Life, Penguin, 1971, p274). Her role as a diplomat signalled her break from revolutionary socialism.

Stalin silenced those who resisted him. Trotsky and his followers were rounded up and sent to prison or exile; 400,000 members of the Bolsheviks were under suspicion. Trotsky lived the rest of his life in exile and until he was murdered by a Stalinist agent in Mexico in 1940. Kollontai was the only leading member of the Bolsheviks to survive Stalin's purges, other than Stalin himself.

Kollontai kept diaries which expressed her disappointment at the declining role of women in the revolution and the regime's loss of "revolutionary humanism" (Farnsworth, p961). However, in public she expressed support for Stalin at crucial moments.

Stalin's priority was to modernise and industrialise the Russian economy as quickly as possible, so that they might have a chance at competing on an international level with the major powers in Europe and the US—especially if there were to be another war. With this in mind, he introduced the first Five Year Plan in 1928. The NEP was over—peasants were forced to collectivise and their grain was requisitioned. The economy was developed at the expense of people's living standards, which plummeted. The state shifted from one based on producing enough to fulfil the needs of the people, to one based on an urgent drive to accumulate capital to feed the arms race with the West.

Russia ceased to be a workers' state, and became instead state capitalist. It was based on exploitation and oppression, at the hands of an all-powerful bureaucracy rather than private capitalists. This complete economic shift dealt the final blow to revolutionary Russia and its most liberating achievements. This was most apparent in the lives of women. The Zhenotdel lost funding and support throughout the 1920s and was shut down in 1932. In 1933 the ban on women working underground and doing night work was ended, and equal pay was overturned. Funding for communal services was cut and women returned to doing housework privately in the home.

Sexual freedom was scorned for being "anti-Marxist" and distracting workers from their roles as producers and mothers. The Stalinist state required more workers, so marriage, the nuclear family and high birth-rates were promoted. Divorce was made too expensive for most people to afford and marriage laws were tightened. Male homosexuality was criminalised. Abortion was banned.

The "joys of motherhood" were promoted by the state. There were cash prizes and medals for women who had five or more children. People were taxed for being single or having too few children.

In 1948 Kollontai wrote an article praising Soviet Russia for providing the conditions which allowed woman to "fulfil her natural duty...to be a mother, the educator of her children and mistress of her home" (Quoted in Holt, p315). These words are a travesty of her earlier writings on the need to liberate women from their oppression in the home.

Kollontai died in Moscow on 9 March 1952, weeks before her 80th birthday. Her greatest achievements lay more than three decades earlier, in her writings and activism and her commitment to women's liberation bound to the revolutionary struggle against capitalism.

★ 18:
THE STRUGGLE
FOR LIBERATION

It is over a century since the working class seized power in 1917, yet the activities and writings of revolutionaries like Alexandra Kollontai are just as relevant today. From Donald Trump in the US to Jair Bolsonaro in Brazil, we face a huge struggle against the sexists, racists and bigots of our time.

Those who see the struggle for liberation as limited to winning formal equality within the institutions of capitalism end up compromising and adapting to the system's priorities. Demands to smash the "glass ceiling" ignore the working class majority contending with the "sticky floor". Today, numerous women sit in top positions in government or in boardrooms. Despite these women leaders, the sources of oppression and exploitation remain in place. Liberation will take more than changing who sits at the top of society.

Every major advance for women over the last 100 years has been linked to the struggle of the working class. Each victory for women workers has also been a victory for the entire working class. The Equal Pay Act in the UK was prompted by the inspiring strike by women seamstresses at Ford Dagenham car plant in 1968. Abortion rights were defended by a mass trade union demonstration in 1979, bringing together female and male workers.

Women workers were at the forefront of the largest strike by public sector workers in British history in

November 2011. Strikes by teachers, mostly women, swept the US in 2018 and 2019, winning significant gains. In autumn 2018 some 8,000 council workers in Glasgow led a historic strike for equal pay.

Working class women led the enormous and historic movement that repealed the 8th Amendment of the Irish constitution in 2018, winning abortion rights.

The 2011 Egyptian revolution saw women help to overthrow the deeply oppressive Mubarak regime. Women have been central to the 2019 revolution in Sudan. However, these uprisings also tell us that socialist revolution is not inevitable. The years following the Egyptian revolution saw a backlash of huge proportions, with the attempt to instil democracy halted by a military regime. The example of the Bolsheviks in 1917 shows the importance of building a revolutionary socialist organisation in advance of a revolution, which can help to defend, guide and secure victory for the working class and the oppressed.

The limited sexual freedoms that women have won over the past few decades have been appropriated by capitalism and sold back to us in the form of "raunch culture". Huge profits are made from turning women's bodies into commodities, whether its adverts asking women to be "beach body ready" or selling pole dancing as a "liberating" form of exercise.

Kollontai's writings on sexual liberation point towards a world where people's relationships are based on more than swiping left or right on a dating app, but are also free from the obligations of economic necessity. She developed a vision of how socialist revolution could open up the possibility of real freedom and liberation for both women and men.

FURTHER READING

Cathy Porter's *Alexandra Kollontai: A Biography* (Merlin Press, 2013) is by far the best account of Kollontai's life, writing and activism.

Porter's *Alexandra Kollontai: Writings From the Struggle* (Haymarket, 2019) makes available a number of newly-translated writings from Kollontai's time in exile in Germany and her years leading the Women's Department in post-revolutionary Russia.

Many of Kollontai's own writings and speeches can be found online at the Marxists Internet Archive, www.marxists.org

Kollontai's short stories and novels bring the Russian Revolution to life. Some of these can be found in *Love of Worker Bees* (Chicago Review Press, 2003), translated by Cathy Porter, afterword by Sheila Rowbotham.

Alix Holt's *Selected Writings of Alexandra Kollontai* (Allison & Busby, 1977) is a wide-ranging collection. It is out of print, but can be found second-hand or in libraries.

Jane McDermid and Anna Hillyar's *Midwives of the Revolution* (UCL, 1999) gives a remarkable account of the lives of working class and peasant women throughout Russia's revolutionary years.

Judith Orr's *Marxism and Women's Liberation* (Bookmarks, 2015) is a fantastic introduction to the argument that puts class at the heart of the struggle for women's liberation.

Leon Trotsky's *The History of the Russian Revolution* (Haymarket, 2008) is the revolutionary's definitive account of the Russian Revolution.

Dave Sherry's *Russia 1917: Workers' Revolution and the Festival of the Oppressed* (Bookmarks, 2017) looks at the history of 1917 from the perspective of socialists in the 21st century.